The Innkeeper
of Bethlehem

The Innkeeper
of Bethlehem

FIRST EDITION

Michael Hume

Yuletime
PUBLISHING COMPANY

COLORADO

The Innkeeper of Bethlehem

ISBN 978-1-956220-66-7 (Hardcover)
ISBN 978-1-956220-68-1 (Digital)

Yuletime Publishing Company
195 South Rancho Vista Drive
Pueblo West, Colorado 81007
www.firewordsmedia.com

Printed in the United States of America

Scriptures are quoted from the Thompson Chain-Reference Bible 4th
Edition (KJV), © 1964 by Kirkbride Bible Co., Inc., and are used with
permission.

Original illustrations by Sherry Olson, SOS Studios, Denver, Colorado

Also by Michael Hume:
The 95th Christmas (literary novel)
The Christmas In Me (musical album)

Look for **The Innkeeper of Bethlehem** in paperback and audiobook,
Christmas 2025

Contents

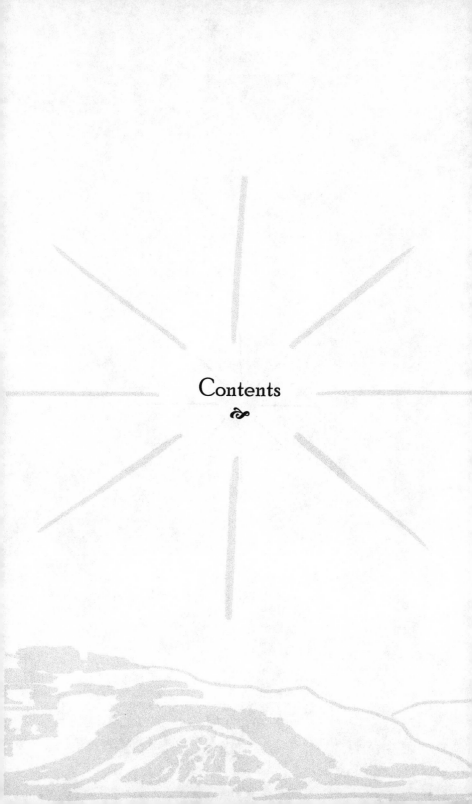

Foreword

In the spirit of currently popular fiction, such as the series *The Chosen*, movies like *Risen* and *The Nativity Story*, and other works, this story is intended as a plausible reimagining of the birth and earthly life of Christ.

The story is not meant to replace Scripture and is not intended to be a work of historical research. As an example of this, fictitious names have been assigned to various Biblical characters in an effort to make those characters real in the imagination of the reader.

Readers are encouraged to read the Scriptures and to imagine how their own personal lives would have been affected had they been blessed to witness the magnificent birth and life of the King of Kings.

I asked my expert illustrator, Sherry Olson, to create images from her own heart based on her reading of the manuscript and to do them in the style of Picasso's *Don Quixote*. I think she nailed it. If anything in the art seems "off," that's my fault for asking for something out of the ordinary, not Sherry's. Thanks, my friend.

My sincere gratitude goes to Caleb DeLon and the entire team at *Paperback Expert* for their help in designing the book and getting it ready for the printers.

My friends at *BNI Action Partners* and *The Original Dickens Carolers* have been gracious in supporting me and supplying me with ideas. Thanks, friends!

Of course, I'm grateful to my wife, Kathryn, and to all of my children and grandchildren for feeding me a steady diet of inspiration. Thanks to you all!

Finally, my deepest gratitude to my longtime friend and counselor, the Reverend John S. McCahan, for giving me a solid "home-churched" grounding in the Word and for glimpses into the mysteries of both this life and the next.

Thank you.

-Michael Hume

Now when Jesus was born in Bethlehem of Judea in the days of Herod the king, behold, there came wise men from the east to Jerusalem,

Saying, where is he that is born King of the Jews? For we have seen his star in the east, and are come to worship him.

When Herod the king had heard these things, he was troubled, and all Jerusalem with him.

And when he had gathered all the chief priests and scribes of the people together, he demanded of them where Christ should be born.

And they said unto him, In Bethlehem of Judaea: for thus it is written by the prophet,

And thou Bethlehem, in the land of Juda, art not the least among the princes of Juda: for out of thee shall come a Governor, that shall rule my people Israel.

Then Herod, when he had privily called the wise men, enquired of them diligently what time the star appeared.

And he sent them to Bethlehem, and said, Go and search diligently for the young child; and when ye have found him, bring me word again, that I may come and worship him also.

When they had heard the king, they departed; and, lo, the star, which they saw in the east, went before them, till it came and stood over where the young child was.

When they saw the star, they rejoiced with exceeding great joy.

From the Gospel of Matthew, Chapter Two

I Three *Obsessions*.

A City in the East… as the Star beckoned.

Gaspar "The Great" was huddled together with his swordsmen against the city's outer wall, which sheltered them somewhat from the gale they could not see, but which tossed the palms about and summoned great piles of sand wherever its whims suggested.

"Lo," said Melchior The Priest, "the wind cannot be seen, but the effects of its labor cannot be missed. Even now, in the darkness of the night."

The swordsmen grunted, and nodded, and Gaspar wondered whether simple men such as these really considered the words of their betters, or merely nodded and grunted to show acquiescence.

He strode to the burdened camel and pulled back the lambskin covering to reveal a gilded box, locked and secured to the beast by sturdy straps.

"I will satisfy your curiosity now and tell you that, yes, this chest is filled with gold coins," Gaspar said, addressing the swordsmen. "They are counted. You will guard this chest, and us, and the rest of our possessions, with your lives. And when we return from our destination, unharmed and unrobbed, you will be richly rewarded. But not from this chest. This is for… this is not for you. This is not for any of us."

The company watched as a sudden gust ripped giant fronds from the nearby palms and sent them sailing like broken birds deep into the night.

The animals brayed, and the swordsmen shifted uneasily on their feet.

"Should we not wait until the storm passes?" Melchior said. "Perhaps in the morning, after a hearty breakfast…"

The swordsmen seemed to welcome this suggestion with what appeared to Gaspar as hopeful glances among their fellows.

"That," Gaspar said, pointing toward the bright Star, "is our beacon. Our guide. It will not be visible in the morning. No, my priestly friend, we must travel at night. Every night. And we must start tonight. We cannot wait."

"We dare not wait," came the soft, low, resonant voice of Balthasar, who was known generally as "The Mystic."

For a long moment, nothing could be heard but the roar and moan of the fierce wind.

"Indeed," Gaspar said. "Let us ride now through this lamentable storm and see if morning might not find us enjoying that meal in the calm on the other side."

And so began the expedition no man among them—from the most noble prince to the most humble servant—would ever forget.

II The *Innkeeper*.

Bethlehem… Late evening… Some thirty years later.
Ben-Jacob was no longer the Innkeeper of Bethlehem. He had passed that honor to his son, Lemuel, a
few years ago, not long after the year of the Census.
But he had placed one crucial condition upon his re-
lease of the business, and so far, Lemuel had honored
it. Ben-Jacob believed his request would be honored
as long as breath remained in him; though tonight,
as he wheezed through the simple task of stoking the
fire in the inn's Great Room, he doubted that would
be much longer.

"What?" Ben-Jacob asked, addressing no one as he placed another stick on the heap and watched the flames reach to lick it. Unable to sleep—as most nights—the old man had the Great Room to himself, while the family and their few guests slumbered and dreamed in their beds.

With some effort, Ben-Jacob straightened himself and slowly made his way toward the heavy wooden front door that, with more effort, he pushed open and stepped through to look at the night.

How different Bethlehem seemed—and yet so much the same—as on that long-ago night that never left his memory, nor, indeed, often strayed very far from his thoughts. The night of the Census... of the overflowing courtyard... of the royalty... and, of course, of the Star.

Tonight, clouds obscured most of the stars, though Ben-Jacob knew they were still up there. He knew with equal certainty that he would never again see anything (anything at all!) to match the miraculous majesty of the Star he had seen that night. A Star it seemed everyone in the world had somehow seen.

The old man sighed and regarded the scene around him with the kind of appraisal one might employ seeing a familiar old friend for the last time. And might that not be the case?

He gazed toward the cloudy heavens and whispered the completion of his question:

"What... is the reason?" he asked no one he could see. "What is the reason I am still here, ancient and infirm, when I should long ago have departed this lowly plain?"

Ben-Jacob heard no answer on the gentle night breeze.

As he pulled his robe tight and turned back toward the fire, he caught a glimpse of two silhouetted figures, some several paces off down the narrow street, slowly making their way toward him. Men, he surmised—one with the steady gait of a man of average age and health, and the other, hooded and more stooped, who seemed much older.

"We seek accommodation," the younger man said, once the pair had reached Ben-Jacob's side. "But first, might we not warm ourselves by the light we see beckoning us through your door?"

Ben-Jacob stood aside and extended his arm in invitation. Three men then stepped inside where he had stepped out just a few moments before.

III Two *Recognitions*.

The Great Room... as the fire hissed and popped.
Once they had helped him push shut the heavy door,
Ben-Jacob regarded more closely the faces of his two
new guests and searched his mind for recognition.
None could be found.

Before he could speak, the younger of the two
men said, "As I live, is it not you, Rabbi? Ben-Jacob?
Still keeping this inn?"

"Do I know you?" Ben-Jacob asked.

"You do not, I think, know the man I am," the stranger replied. "But search your memory, and you may recall the boy I was."

Ben-Jacob peered intently at the man's face, but could find no memory of him. But he was able to answer his question thus, "Yes, I am Ben-Jacob, but many years have passed since I turned the keeping of the inn over to my son. I no longer keep much, other than this fire. And those things I can no longer keep include the better part of my memory, I am afraid, so if you and I were acquainted in the past, you shall have to remind me of it."

"I am Dimasz," the stranger said, grasping Ben-Jacob's shoulder. (Instinctively, and as custom suggested, Ben-Jacob clapped his own hand on Dimasz's shoulder, returning the friendly gesture of greeting.) "I was but a young boy... a boy of twelve, I believe?... when we first met."

The old man's gaze lingered a moment on Dimasz's face, still searching for any hint of familiarity. Then, as he felt the old habit of hospitality directing him, he turned to greet the other stranger.

"I am Ben-Jacob, father of the Innkeeper," he said, reaching to grasp the stooped shoulder of the man.

The man smiled but said nothing. He seemed to look Ben-Jacob in the eye, but next moment, it seemed to Ben-Jacob as though the stranger was not really seeing him, but perhaps gazing past the sound of his voice, as a blind man might.

The bent old stranger shuffled past Ben-Jacob, seemingly bound by singular urgency toward a seat near the fire's warmth.

"I am not certain how he is called," Dimasz told Ben-Jacob, as they watched the man feel his way to the seat. "I am also not sure he has full use of his senses. I have not heard him utter a word, nor have I been convinced he sees or hears what is happening in the world around him. He seems to have another world to himself. But then," Dimasz paused, with a slight smile in his voice, "I guess I have not known him long."

"How long?" Ben-Jacob asked.

"You could say we met within the hour," the young man said. "I was making my way to you, and as I passed the wall of the town, I was joined by this poor unfortunate. We walked along in silence, and at length I asked if he wanted accommodation, and if he might care to join me on my visit to your inn. He nodded, and we continued to your door."

Ben-Jacob scarcely gathered the last of Dimasz's words before he stretched an arm in welcome toward the seats near the fire. The two men moved to join the old stranger there.

Once all were seated, Ben-Jacob renewed his quest for recognition. "Tell me, please," he said, "as you are correct in saying that I do not recognize the man you are… how did I have occasion to meet the boy you were, all those years ago?"

"Some two-score years ago, I think," Dimasz said, with a relaxed sigh. "I was tending my family's flock nearby one afternoon—you may recall, that was the year of the great journeys—of The Great Census—when my eye beheld a most amazing sight. It was a small caravan of camels, and soldiers, and high-born men dressed in the finest raiment. For the price of a shiny coin, I was pressed into their service and all but abandoned our fine flock to run ahead into town. To the inn. To you, Reb' Ben-Jacob! To announce the impending arrival—."

"You do not mean to say—."

"Yes, Rabbi," Dimasz said. "It was I who bade you make room in your inn for The Great Gaspar, prince of the east, and for his venerated company."

IV First *Memory*.

By the merry fire… and also in the hallway of Recollection.

"Rabbi" Ben-Jacob, the old Innkeeper of Bethlehem, was neither Innkeeper now nor, in the strictest sense, a rabbi. But nevertheless, he appreciated young Dimasz's use of this title of respect.

He made fleeting note of the courtesy. But more intently, as Ben-Jacob stared into the flicker of the flames on his hearth, his mind bent itself backward to recall the experience to which Dimasz had just referred… the beginning of the experience that marked that long-ago night as one that would forever be etched in his heart.

A long moment stretched itself silently through the Great Room, and then: "Yes," Ben-Jacob said, his voice very near a whisper, "it was early in the afternoon. Just past the midday meal. I remember," he said, a touch of wonder giving a slight rise to his tone, "somehow… I remember it all."

Dimasz placed his hand on Ben-Jacob's arm, and the old man felt a friendliness in it. "Will you favor us?" Dimasz asked. "Favor us, please, with the memory? I am sure we would appreciate even the smallest detail."

Ben-Jacob's gaze returned to the flames, and his mind returned to that long-ago afternoon. He drew an old man's breath, and then he spoke of his recollection of events.

"Lemuel and his wife had been helping with the chores since before the sun rose," he said. "Their young children were busy at play in the inn-yard. They lived in Jerusalem in those days, but of course, the Census decree had brought them here to be assessed. We had many other guests, too. Business was good! The Census had been a boon for us."

Ben-Jacob glanced at his visitors. The bent stranger sat in a slump, his chin low upon his chest, and Ben-Jacob could not discern whether he was still among the living, let alone listening to his tale. But Dimasz was watching intently and seemed to hold close every word.

"We had just finished serving the midday meal with its wine, and Rubel—she was the whore of the inn in those days—had just arisen, living as she did on her own schedule, and was just breaking her fast. Business was brisk. Remarkably so! I do remember that. The inn was nearly full already that midday. But apart from that fact, up to that time, it was life as usual."

Ben-Jacob sat staring at the flames for another long moment; then, as if jolted from a dream, he suddenly turned to regard Dimasz. "Then the boy—then you!—burst through the open doorway with the great proclamation. My inn was to be visited by kings! Not just one, but three! Along with an entire entourage of servants and swordsmen, and several weary beasts of burden. All here! In *my* inn! What an excitement. What an honor!"

"Was it?" Dimasz asked.

Ben-Jacob gave a small laugh. "But, of course," he said. "I remember like it was mere moments ago. So I set about preparing accommodation for my most-honored guests. The most important guests in the long history of the inn!"

The old Innkeeper smiled at the memory. But it was Dimasz's turn to laugh.

"You remember, like it was mere moments ago," Dimasz said.

"Indeed."

"So, what is it you recall?" Dimasz pressed.

"What feeling, on receiving this joyous unexpected news, did you experience?"

V Making Room.

In the next moment, and in song.

What is it we cherish? What gives us delight?

What fills us with pride as we blow out the light?

What fills us, indeed! For is that not our aim?

To fill ourselves up; is that not our game?

For each of us here's like an inn on the plains

And we stuff ourselves full until no room remains

'Tis the way of all flesh; we will always make room

For the things we think treasures...

... We will ALWAYS make room.

Dimasz sang these words in a low, clear voice, and when he had done, he addressed the old Innkeeper of Bethlehem with a supposition biting, even wounding in its content, but with a calm tone that evoked a mysterious comfort in Ben-Jacob.

You felt delight, no doubt, and great pride at the news that you would host these men of high regard. You hastened—no? Ah, but how you hastened to make room in your inn for these important guests.

And who—or what—occupied your inn already? Customers: those who had money to pay. Some of them had kin of their own in Bethlehem, for they had been sent "home" by the Census. Had they not? Yet they preferred to take rooms in your inn.

Your own offspring were here too, of course. And, no doubt, there were less "honorable" guests. You had made room for the harlot to ply her trade within your inn— you mentioned it yourself. And who knows what other blackguards had taken up residence inside your walls... dark figures with evil errands known only to their own shadowed hearts? Pickpockets? Highwaymen? Young thieves?

A tear made its way down Ben-Jacob's creased cheek. At length, his gaze moved from the flames to the face of his young guest.

"What should I have done?" he asked, as much of himself as of Dimasz. "What *could* I have done any differently? It is the business. Business was good!"

The old man turned back to the fire, and whispered again: "Business was good."

Dimasz leaned forward, plucked a small stick from the pile on the hearth, and added it to the fire. He sat back with a sigh.

"Who knows?" Dimasz said. "Who knows what you could have done? I am sure you have always been an innkeeper like any other. No worse. No better. Perhaps you think yourself good. And perhaps it is not important. Perhaps what you do *now* is the important thing."

"I can do nothing now," Ben-Jacob quickly said, with a snort.

After a silence, the old man addressed Dimasz again.

"Who *are* you?"

Dimasz met his gaze. "I am Dimasz, son of Abrim, and I have been a thief my whole life. As it happens, I was one of the young blackguards staying here that night, and having been seduced by a gold coin, I began a life of skullduggery, right here, in this now-crumbling house, all those years ago. But be not alarmed, Rabbi. I came here tonight not to rob you again, but to repay you."

Ben-Jacob said nothing in reply.

The old, slumped-over stranger did not stir and offered no comment.

VI The *King*.

Jerusalem, in the days of the Star's first appearance.
Herod was a king like any other in his day. No worse.
No better. That is to say, he was a ruthless, power-
hungry tyrant.

But Herod was a king in an occupied land. King,
but not ruler. Enthroned, but hardly empowered. He
was a man who lived an easy life, but he had no real
authority. Of this, he was constantly reminded by the
governors Rome sent to rule over his people and to

keep Herod and the other Jews of any standing in their easy, comfortable cages.

And to "keep the peace," in the way peace is always kept by tyrants: at the point of the spear.

Being constantly reminded of the reality of his position unsurprisingly made Herod a most political man. He keenly felt how little real power he had, and he lived in a continuous state of wariness that, at times, grew to a sort of fear that bordered on terror. As with many men whom fate has favored with a little something, it was worry over the possible loss of that little something that ruled Herod even more firmly than did his Roman masters.

Perhaps it was this fear, this constant gnawing worry, which was the true reason for the declaration of The Great Census. The Romans ordered the Census, to be sure. But might Herod not have whispered the thought into the right Roman ears? And it was a most shrewd decision, benefiting all sides. The Romans would have the Hebrews too busy journeying across the land to make much progress with the bothersome rebellions that afflicted this part of Caesar's realm like a low fever. And Herod would draw this "messiah" usurper to Bethlehem, where he could be found and stamped out like a sparking ember that would never bring forth a flame.

The timing was perfect. Caiphas and other Pharisee "holy men" had been warning for weeks that the time was drawing nigh for the rise of this usurper, as foretold by their ancient predecessors. And now there were rumors of a small caravan of princes from the east—wise and powerful men who had already left their own thrones to make the perilous trek to Bethlehem to give to this upstart the respect and homage Herod knew should have been *his,* all along.

The king summoned his son, Antipas, with the intention to charge him with seeing to things. Which is to say, to make sure Antipas knew that any future kingdom he might enjoy would depend on finding this usurper in Bethlehem.

And killing him.

And it came to pass in those days that there went out a decree from Caesar Augustus, that all the world should be taxed.

And all went to be taxed, every one to his own city.

And Joseph also went up from Galilee, out of the city of Nazareth, into Judaea, unto the city of David, which is called Bethlehem; (because he was of the house and lineage of David:)

… To be taxed with Mary his espoused wife, being great with child.

And so it was, that, while they were there, the days were accomplished that she should be delivered.

And she brought forth her firstborn son, and wrapped him in swaddling clothes, and laid him in a manger; because there was no room for them in the inn.

And there were in the same country shepherds abiding in the field, keeping watch over their flock by night.

And, lo, the angel of the Lord came upon them, and the glory of the Lord shone round about them: and they were sore afraid.

And the angel said unto them, Fear not: for, behold, I bring you good tidings of great joy, which shall be to all people.

For unto you is born this day in the city of David a Saviour, which is Christ the Lord.

And this shall be a sign unto you; Ye shall find the babe wrapped in swaddling clothes, lying in a manger.

And suddenly there was with the angel a multitude of the heavenly host praising God, and saying,

Glory to God in the highest, and on earth peace, good will toward men.

From the Gospel of Luke, Chapter Two

And when [the wise men] were come into the house, they saw the young child with Mary his mother, and fell down, and worshipped him: and when they had opened their treasures, they presented unto him gifts; gold, and frankincense and myrrh.
And being warned of God in a dream that they should not return to Herod, they departed into their own country another way.

From the Gospel of Matthew, Chapter Two

VII The *Arrival.*

Bethlehem, the day and Holy Night.

Gaspar The Great had prepared his mind for a difficult journey and for a destination that would lack the comfort to which he had been accustomed all his life. The journey had not disappointed his low expectations; his first appraisal of Bethlehem, and its inn, was even lower than he had expected.

The Innkeeper had made his best room available to Gaspar, and from this choice location just off the

Great Room, he could hear the keeper turning away beggar after beggar at the door. Even Melchior and Balthazar had to climb ladders to lesser rooms, but they were still afforded the best hospitality the poor Innkeeper could manage, in accordance with their noble status. And the swordsmen and servants seemed comfortable enough in the courtyard.

The Innkeeper had served them the best meal he could produce, but Gaspar could only reminisce about the royal banquet they had enjoyed in the palace of Herod, just two nights earlier. Now, as the three princes were finishing the humble supper they had been served, Gaspar asked the Innkeeper where he might find the newborn king.

"You are the only kings with whom I am acquainted this night, Your Grace," the keeper had said. "As for a newborn, we might find one in the stable, since that is where I sent the couple I had to turn away just now. A most desperate man and his very-pregnant wife. But they hardly had the look of royalty, so I doubt it will be any kind of king they will deliver."

Nevertheless, upon Gaspar's request, the Innkeeper guided the three princes down the lane to his stable, where they found a small gathering of peasants who had collected themselves at the stable's entrance—at the very spot where the Star had settled and where it now shone the brightest light any of them had ever seen.

Gaspar and his companions made their way through the gathering, and when they saw the ragged little family, each noble king fell to his knees, forever changed. For they saw the light of the Star reflecting powerfully from the mother and father... and they saw what each man could only describe as the Light of Heaven emanating from the tiny child Himself.

Gaspar quickly rose, and he turned away. He saw that his manservant had followed him to the stable and had brought his camel along. Gaspar dashed to the animal, loosed the straps, and brought forth the chest of gold.

"I brought this to pay tribute, to form a trading alliance with the new king of the land," he said as he set the chest beside the infant's manger-crib. "Now, I see this gold should have been a gift. A true gift from my heart, to the King of kings."

Melchior the Priest followed. "I thought I might meet the high priest of this new kingdom, and that our two religions might finally become one, with grand rituals during which this fine aroma might fill the air," he said. "Now, I see that I have met the Priest of all priests, and this gift of rarest frankincense belongs here, at His side."

Balthazar, the "Mystic," simply presented his gift of myrrh, without explaining why he had chosen to give this herb of embalming for one's honored dead. Instead, he addressed his fellow princes thus:

"After weeks of following the Star, did we expect to reach the Star itself? What *did* we expect? The wise should know that the stars that attract us to follow them are but signposts. We are attracted not by the thing that shines, but by the Light of Heaven that the thing reflects."

Then, Balthazar raised his deep voice in song:

When we dined with Herod
The silver was arrayed
With tablecloths of linen
Where plates of gold were laid.
We feasted to contentment,
The wine so freely flowed.
We could have stayed with Herod,
But we took a different road.

In Bethlehem, we might have sought
A palace, and a queen,

But a stable and a virgin
Are the only things we've seen.
We might have sought alliance
With a mighty worldly king
But instead, received a blessing,
And beheld the King of kings.

In Bethlehem, we found it,
The Thing we came to see
But not as we expected,
Not one among us three.
We could have dined with Herod,
But won't return again.
We'll go a different way, for now
We go as different men.

VIII The *Peace.*

Bethlehem, on the Holy Night.

Gaspar, the "Great" king, employed a manservant whose name has been lost to all memory. Though history has never recorded it, even people such as this servant were forever changed by the Birth he witnessed that night.

He certainly thought himself a humble man, but in truth, he was filled with great pride of his position as the king's manservant. After all, many poor men were pressed into the service of other men who enjoyed greater means… but not all servants were afforded a small room in the palace of the king, along with which came better food, and better raiment, than other servants ever knew. Being named the personal manservant to the king himself was no small honor.

From his makeshift bed in the inn-yard, the manservant, along with the swordsmen and the rest of the company, beheld in hushed awe the scene in the stable, some forty paces away. He, along with the others, saw the breathtaking light of the Star, and could also discern the light emanating from the manger, as though Something of Earth was shining in bright answer to the Light of Heaven.

When he saw the Innkeeper leading his master and the other princes toward the stable, Gaspar's manservant leapt to his feet and scurried to fetch the king's camel. He found himself joined by several others, including the manservants of the other princes, and many of the swordsmen (but not all).

Gaspar's manservant followed with his prince's animal a few paces behind the royal company; when he drew close enough himself to behold the newborn Child, the manservant fell to his knees in solemn worship, just as had everyone else who had arrived on the scene.

The manservant could hear the soft voices of the princes as they offered their gifts to this strange young family. He heard the voices but could make out none of the words. As the light shone, and the voices began to fade, the manservant bade the camel sit, and he himself soon did the same.

At length, the manservant became aware of a wonderful sound that must have been singing, but though he had been fortunate enough to hear the king's minstrel chorus serenading the royal court on more than one occasion, this was a sound of singing unlike, and vastly superior to, any he had heard before. Whether it was this odd and beautiful sound, or the gentle brightness of the Star's light, or the outpouring from heart to heart of what he could only describe as mighty unspoken Love, a calm serenity appeared to overwhelm everyone present. At last, it seemed everyone had fallen into the deepest, most peaceful sleep.

He may not have discerned it. Certainly, he would have had no moment of sharp realization. But as the blessed event overwhelmed him, Gaspar's manservant was emptied of all worldly pride and care, and filled—at least for a time—with Love, Joy, and Peace.

He might have felt as though these things were born not only in the manger before him but in the soul within him.

* * *

At this time, in distant Jerusalem, no singing could be heard. But the light of the Star was unmistakable, and anyone who beheld it even from a distance knew that something extraordinary was surely taking place.

Every Hebrew child had been taught God's history of miracles, from the Divine acts in the days of Abraham, to the great flood of the days of Noah, to the pillar of fire that had led the people to the promised land. Therefore all would have known that a Star such as this one was not beyond the power of God's making.

But what was the meaning of this new miracle?

Antipas, son of King Herod, Prince of Israel, also beheld this Light from Heaven, and of course he had also learned the history of God's miracles. He knew that many in Jerusalem, and especially many of the most learned, would interpret this Star as a herald of their long-awaited Messiah. But Antipas had been taught, from a very early age, that he himself would one day rise to lead his people against the brutal rule of the Romans, and that, as far as anyone could tell, he himself would be the savior of the nation.

Antipas interpreted the Star to be a herald, as did many in Jerusalem. But he assumed himself to be the heralded one, and the Star to be a sign from God that his own kingdom was nigh. But could it be through the slaughter of Hebrew children that his rise was to be accomplished?

"Remember that Elijah slew the four hundred and fifty prophets of Baal," whispered Morchai, his young friend, in Antipas's ear. "Who are we to judge the mysterious designs of God?"

Antipas considered this. God had, indeed, in times past, ordered violence against the enemies of his chosen people. Might this distasteful violence, ordered by his father as God's anointed king, be no different from the cleansing slaughters of the past?

He sighed and turned to Morchai.

"Assemble your men," he said.

And when [the wise men] were departed, behold, the angel of the Lord appeareth to Joseph in a dream, saying, Arise, and take the young child and his mother, and flee into Egypt, and be thou there until I bring thee word: for Herod will seek the young child to destroy him.

When he arose, he took the young child and his mother by night, and departed into Egypt:

And was there until the death of Herod: that it might be fulfilled which was spoken of the Lord by the prophet, saying, Out of Egypt have I called my son.

Then Herod, when he saw that he was mocked of the wise men, was exceeding wroth, and sent forth, and slew all the children that were in Bethlehem, and in all the coasts thereof, from two years old and under...

... Then was fulfilled that which was spoken by Jeremiah the prophet, saying,

In Rama was there a voice heard, lamentation, and weeping, and great mourning, Rachel weeping for her children, and would not be comforted, because they are not.

From the Gospel of Matthew, Chapter Two

IX The *Innocents*.

Bethlehem, when they least expected it.

Many believed, when they learned of the ghastly
slaughter of Bethlehem's innocent young boys, that
it was a band of Roman soldiers who had carried out
the heinous deed. Such brutality surely would not
have been out of character for Caesar's legions. But
in fact, the Roman commanders had never had much
interest in the mythology of the people they had
conquered. A Hebrew "Messiah" posed no threat to

Rome. No, they were Hebrew swordsmen—subjects of Rome whose allegiance was to the king of Israel—who slaughtered the Innocents.

As the murderous platoon was riding toward Bethlehem, Ben-Jacob and the others who had been blessed to witness the Holy Birth were stirring from a slumber of which none of them could reckon the duration. For his part, Ben-Jacob surmised from the sore ache of his joints that he had slept at least a day, and perhaps two. Who could truly tell? But when he woke, the noble company of Gaspar and his royal companions was well along in their preparations for departure. And the young family he had sent to give Birth in his stable was long gone.

"They left in the night," Gaspar told Ben-Jacob. "The father thanked us for our gifts, but told us an angel of God had appeared to him in a dream and bade him flee in haste with the Child and His mother. His beast could not bear the burden of the gifts. I offered him as many camels as he would need, and indeed, swordsmen to guard his journey. But he insisted that he must travel fast and light, and must do everything possible not to draw attention. So we filled his purse with coins and watched as he and his young family hurried from Bethlehem in much the same way they had come."

As he heard these words, Ben-Jacob became aware of the presence of his son, Lemuel, who had drawn nigh. "So what is to become of the gold—that is, what is to become of the gifts left behind?" Lemuel asked. "And might we not expect remuneration for our hospitality? After all, Your Grace, this is our family's sole business."

"Pshah!" Ben-Jacob exclaimed. "Lemuel, now is not the time…"

"Nay, your son is correct," Gaspar said. "We will leave the gold, and the incense, and the herbs, with you. Take what you believe is fair, for your own exertions," he said. "And keep the rest, in case He should ever return."

"In case who should return?" Lemuel asked.

"Why, the Divine Child!" Gaspar said.

With that, Gaspar and his company departed Bethlehem and were never again seen within the borders of Israel or Judea.

* * *

Ben-Jacob would not have known it, but a young Hebrew called Morchai had been chosen to lead the company of Herod's soldiers, despite his youth and inexperience. Morchai had but sixteen or seventeen years, but his blood lust was well known in the court of Herod. He had been called upon to perform many tasks for Herod and Antipas that other soldiers would have found distasteful for their sheer meanness.

Gaspar's company had scarcely cleared the city walls when Ben-Jacob saw Herod's martial company ride swiftly into Bethlehem. "Slay every male with two years or fewer," he heard the young commander cry. "We must be absolutely certain!"

And so the dreadful slaughter began.

Ben-Jacob ran to defend his own grandson, Lemuel's son Timoth. But a young soldier cast the Innkeeper aside, drew his sword, and prepared to strike the little child.

At that moment, the soldier paused. Ben-Jacob would later say he had caught a look of sadness, perhaps regret, which appeared for a long moment on the young swordsman's face. And when the soldier hesitated, Morchai, commander of the troops, strode forward and beheaded the soldier with a single blow.

Then Morchai slew Timoth without delay.

* * *

The Innkeeper was wailing in the street, as were many others. Through his tears, Ben-Jacob saw Dimasz, the young shepherd boy, scurrying from the inn.

He carried the gilded chest and what was left of the gold.

"Return to Herod, and to the prince!" Ben-Jacob heard the young commander shout. As the other soldiers rode away, Morchai drew his sword across Dimasz's throat.

"Where do you think you are going?" he demanded of the boy.

"Why, to Your Grace," Dimasz said, after but a blink of hesitation. "Just look, and behold what riches I have recovered for you!"

Morchai smiled.

X The *Reflection*.

The Great Room.

As he finished reflecting on the tragedy he experienced in Bethlehem on that fateful day, Ben-Jacob looked up to see a solitary tear making its way down Dimasz's face.

"Now I remember you," Ben-Jacob said. "Of course. It was you who stole the gold and rode away on the back of a horse. The horse of that... that murderer."

"As I said," Dimasz managed, "I had let myself become seduced."

Dimasz drew a deep, ragged breath, then raised his voice again in song.

Gold is but a thing that shines
It makes itself no light
In fact it looks as any stone
When viewed in darkest night.

> *All upon the Earth is stone*
> *From golden coin to flesh and bone*
> *Nothing is itself complete*
> *And nothing shines alone.*

Life is wasted when spent seeking
Naught but stones of Earth,
Earthly rocks can bring no life
And stones can give no birth.

> *I know this, yet I saw the Light*
> *Born in flesh upon that night*
> *But even so, I turned away*
> *And hid my eyes from sight.*

All my life I scrapped for gold
But gathered only stone
I sought to steal the wealth of men
But did my soul disown.

> *Far from Hope I sought to roam*
> *And late regarded what I'd done*
> *I cried out in my final hour*
> *And Mercy brought me home.*

Dimasz's voice cracked to a shredded whisper as he sang the last. He now wept, deeply, his face cradled in his hands.

Ben-Jacob, ever the gracious host, hastened to fetch a cup of water from a nearby stone basin. When he turned to hand the cup to Dimasz, he saw something that terrified him so that he dropped the cup, shattering it to shards upon the stone floor.

"Your... your arms!" Ben-Jacob gasped. "You are wounded! Harshly wounded through each wrist! How... why..?"

"We were a team," Dimasz said, quickly pulling his sleeves back over his hands and using them to dry his face. "Morchai and I. We became a fell team of thieves that day."

Ben-Jacob slowly sat, his gaze fixed upon the hems of Dimasz's sleeves, though the wounds that had startled him were no longer visible. "A team of thieves," the old man whispered.

"Yes," Dimasz continued, his voice plain and matter-of-fact to Ben-Jacob's mind. "From his position in the government of Herod, and later of Antipas, Morchai was able to learn many things that appealed to the designs of a thief. Which visitors to the city had money, and where they kept it. Who was traveling alone, or nearly alone, along which deserted roads. Where the best and easiest prey could be taken."

"And you were the taker? You, but a boy?"

"A boy at first, but soon, a narrow man who had spent his life in training for stealth. When it was stealth that was needed, Morchai relied upon me. When more direct, violent action was required, I relied upon him. As I say, we were a team, and a very successful team at that."

"But… then… what happened to..?"

"The money?" What happened to all that money?" Dimasz issued a dark laugh. "What indeed!"

Dimasz leaned forward.

"I will tell you what happened," he said, meeting Ben-Jacob's eyes with an unblinking gaze of his own. "We indulged our every lust. Women. Feasting. All the best wine. Morchai and I—we were the life of every party!"

He laughed again, meanly, as if mocking himself. "The life!" Dimasz said. "What a jest. Yes, we were the 'life.' Right up to the wicked night when we were caught, and tried, and justly sentenced to death."

And there were also two other, malefactors, led with him to be put to death.

And when they were come to the place, which is called Calvary, there they crucified him, and the malefactors, one on the right hand, and the other on the left.

…And one of the malefactors which were hanged railed on him, saying, If thou be Christ, save thyself and us.

But the other answering rebuked him, saying, Dost not thou fear God, seeing thou art in the same condemnation?

And we indeed justly; for we receive the due reward of our deeds: but this man hath done nothing amiss.

And he said unto Jesus, Lord, remember me when thou comest into thy kingdom.

And Jesus said unto him, Verily I say unto thee, Today shalt thou be with me in paradise.

From the Gospel of Luke, Chapter Twenty-Three

XI The Crosses.

The Great Room, as the fire began to die.

"Death!" Ben-Jacob gasped. "How did you escape?"

Dimasz managed a weak laugh through anguished weeping. "None of us escapes Death," he said.

Ben-Jacob, stunned beyond words, sank back on his seat. His questions lodged in his throat, but they showed plainly forth on his wrinkled face.

"I will tell you what happened," Dimasz said. "I will tell you all. I believe that is why I am here. The truth unfolded over years, and on this wise."

I was a bad shepherd. One glimpse of a golden coin persuaded my wicked young heart to abandon my flock, and to leave my family, and to seek a worldly fortune, however I could come by it. I considered returning to the shepherd's field that night (and should have!), but I discarded the idea in favor of learning what great goings-on had drawn kings to this town.

When the servants and many of the swordsmen left the inn-yard to witness what Light shone from the stable, I decided only late to follow them. By the time I arrived, I could draw no closer than the back of the crowd. But I arrived in time to see the treasure of gold laid beside a shining Babe. I heard the voice of a shepherd, a man I knew, telling one of the swordsmen that this was exactly what he had expected to find—a swaddled Babe lying in a manger—because an angel had appeared to all in the shepherd's field to announce that this was a newborn Savior, Christ the Lord, and that this is how he would be found.

I did not believe his word. I had seen no angel. No Heavenly glory had shone 'round about me. Nay, I only believed what I had seen with my own eyes—and only the unimportant things, at that. Yea, I had seen a Babe shining with unearthly Light, but I understood it not. I had seen the gold. That, I understood. That, I believed.

I grew bored, and I fell asleep. When I woke next morning, the gold had been moved to the king's room in the inn. I assumed he meant to take it back, since he could not have expected they would be peasants to whom he had been led by the Star. But when he and the rest of his company left Bethlehem, behold, they left the gold behind! The very thing I sought was now within reach, unguarded, and I reckoned I had no less right to such an abandoned treasure as had anyone else.

As you witnessed, and as you may recall, I soon understood that I must needs share the gold with Herod's captain—with the man I came to know as Morchai. And when I told you that Morchai's position in the government gave great advantage to our criminal enterprise, I am sure I will have understated that advantage. Morchai was granted complete freedom to take whatever he wanted, and to kill whoever he wanted, as long as he was always also at the service of the king for whatever nefarious deed the king required. Morchai was untouchable. And, as his faithful accomplice, so was I.

But those who dwell always and only in the world of the political, and who put their faith therein, are destined to fall when the winds change, as they always do. I learned it too late. And so did Morchai.

For instance, as Herod lay dying, he learned of an uprising during which some young Jews sought to remove a graven image from the temple—one that Herod himself had erected in homage to Rome. The rebels were caught, and Herod ordered them burned alive for their insurrection. Can you guess who lit the pyre? It was my "friend," Morchai.

Herod died nonetheless—none of us escapes Death, as I said—and Morchai's friend Antipas was elevated. Antipas, too, though, soon saw his power diminished as Rome set him aside in favor of Caesar's own selected governors—powerful political men such as Pilate.

And when "Herod Antipas" diminished, so did Morchai. He lost his "untouchable" status. When younger versions of himself rose through Rome's ranks, they sought Morchai's downfall, and his days of freedom were numbered. His life of crime finally caught up with him. And I was caught up with him as well.

We watched as the Nazarene was flogged nearly to death, Morchai and I, and I was stunned when Morchai declared that the man was getting his just punishment. He was a usurper, Morchai said, and deserved death for defying the crown.

I was surprised at Morchai's fealty to the crown that would shortly put us both to a painful death, but I was even more surprised at what I came to realize about my own life. I had been a bad shepherd, but I would now be crucified alongside The Good Shepherd—the One who would lead his people, ALL people, as wayward sheep, to redemption.

I suddenly realized, in that same moment, who I truly was. I was a man like any other. No worse. No better. That is to say, I had become a man who chose always to believe only in what he wanted, despite even his own Divine experiences.

I was a thief as well, of course, and I realized we are all thieves, stealing the spirit God gives us for his Divine purposes and using it for our own. What debts we sinners owe to Him from whom we've stolen so much!

And now, here on the cross beside mine, was my only Hope, and the only Hope for us all. I hadn't believed it when I'd seen his Heavenly presence with my own eyes, as he lay shining in the manger on that long-ago night. But now I knew that the words of my fellow shepherds had been true. Every word. Here was God made flesh, willing to forgive us, and willing to pay our debts with his own precious Life.

"We were crucified, the three of us, and when I summoned the courage to confess myself to the Nazarene, He told me I would be with him in Paradise," Dimasz said.

"But I find myself here," he said. "Is Bethlehem Paradise? I think not. I think perhaps this is but a sojourn on my way to that blessed place.

"Am I to tarry the night in that room I see—the one where a candle glows and incense burns in soft invitation?"

XII The Room.

The Inn of Bethlehem.

Dimasz rose, and stretched himself, and began to make his way toward the empty room he saw just off the Great Room. The room where he knew Gaspar had slept, so many years ago. The best room in the house.

"Nay," Ben-Jacob said, as he rose, unhurriedly, and moved to block the room. "This room has been reserved for many years. No one has been given accommodation here, ever since... ever since that night. I bade my son Lemuel to hold this room reserved, all these years, in case the Child born in Bethlehem on that long-ago night should return. And my son promised he would honor that request until the day I drew my last breath."

"Your request has been fulfilled, I think," said Dimasz. "One has come to claim the reservation."

Ben-Jacob reached to clasp Dimasz's shoulder. "Am I to believe all of this?" he asked. "That a resurrected, crucified man such as yourself—a thief, who was once a wayward shepherd boy—would come at last to claim this room I've guarded so long? This room I swore I would never again allow to be occupied by anyone, even a worldly king, against the possibility that the King of kings would one day return to claim it? For that is the oath I swore to Almighty God, the day the soldiers killed my grandson. Never again, I swore, would I displace the Godly in favor of the worldly!"

Just then, the hooded stranger rose with unexpected spryness from his seat by the dying fire. He removed his hood, and Ben-Jacob beheld an unearthly Light in His eyes. He raised His hands in a gesture of warmth and love, and as the sleeves of His robe fell away, Ben-Jacob beheld the same wounds on His wrists that he'd seen on Dimasz.

"This is He," Dimasz said, "for whom you have saved the best room in your house. But, as it happens, He goes now to prepare a place for you in the Heavenly mansion of His Father, despite the fact that you failed to make a place for Him on that long-ago night. For that is the nature of God's grace. He wants all of His children to come home to Him. Even late-penitent thieves. Even bad shepherds. Even lowly innkeepers. For God knows all of us are keepers, each of an earthly 'inn,' and He also knows we are wroth to leave room in our inns for anyone or anything not of our own design. Even for the Lord Himself."

Each of us is granted a place, from God on high,
A place wherein our soul can dwell while Earthly life goes by
And God dwells in there with us, e'er since His Son was born,
For we are but an Earthly cloak the Lord of all has worn.

> *We strive to fill ourselves*
> *With treasures of our own design*
> *And squeeze away the room*

That should be saved for the Divine.
We keep the mean, and leave the good;
The hate, and leave the Love,
But 'twas never room in the inn 'twas sought,
But room in the keeper thereof.

Dimasz sang these words in solemn, gentle tones. Once he had finished, he made his way to the heavy wooden door, and he pushed it open.

Ben-Jacob understood.

Three men then stepped outside the Inn of Bethlehem, where all three had stepped inside just a short time before.

* * *

When Lemuel rose, he was surprised to find the fire in the Great Room had died stone-cold. And he found no trace of his father, Ben-Jacob.

The humble stable, and the manger, will never be forgotten. But in time, all memory was lost of the inn that once housed venerated wise men from the East, and swordsmen, and shepherds, and weary travelers from throughout Israel and Judea.

And no one, save the Most High, has any memory of the Innkeeper of Bethlehem.

About the *Author*

Michael Hume is a freelance writer, singer, and songwriter and serves as regional director of The Original Dickens Carolers. He's an honor graduate of the Defense Information School and holds an M.S. from the University of Colorado School of Business in Denver.

Michael has worked as a journalist, U.S. paratrooper, carpenter, newspaper editor, telephone operator, actor, singer, director, janitor, graphic artist, salesman, laborer, consultant, speaker, teacher, executive coach, counselor, manager, blogger, and entrepreneur. He's accumulated more than a million airline miles.

On the bookshelves in his office, you'd find the complete works of Martin Luther, as well as those of Abraham Lincoln. On the piano in his studio, you'd see a few scratchy, hand-written lead sheets from some of the 200-or-so songs he's penned. In his side of the fridge, you'd find lots of protein but very few carbs. You'd see reminders of the Denver Broncos, Colorado Rockies, Christmas, and Don Quixote all over the house... and in the backyard, you'd see the fire pit and stone benches where he and his wife like to enjoy the blazing western sunsets they're blessed to witness nearly every evening.

Michael lives in Colorado with his wonderful wife, Kathryn, and their beloved dog, Poppins.

The Innkeeper
of Bethlehem

The Innkeeper
of Bethlehem

FIRST EDITION

Michael *Hume*

PUBLISHING COMPANY

COLORADO

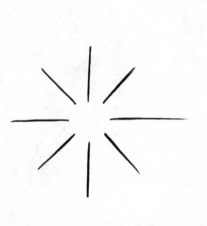